W9-BRQ-953

ALL ABOARD!
A TRUE TRAIN STORY

WORDS AND PHOTOGRAPHS BY **SUSAN KUKLIN**

ORCHARD BOOKS ♦ NEW YORK

The five Durango & Silverton Narrow Gauge steam engines in this story are still in operation today. They were photographed at various locations along their route in the Colorado Rocky Mountains.

All aboard! Turn the page and step back to a time when narrow gauge steam engines clickety-clacked along the historic San Juan wilderness.

Ring the bell
All Aboard!

WHOO-
WHOO

Ready to go

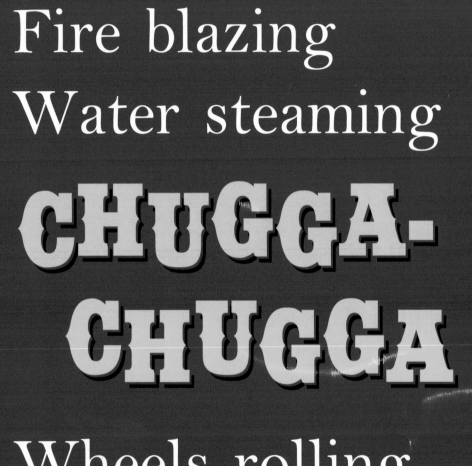

Fire blazing
Water steaming

CHUGGA-
CHUGGA

Wheels rolling

Lights blinking
Signs warning
CLICKETY-CLACK
Railroad crossing

Along the track
CHUGGA-CHUGGA

CLICKETY-CLACK

Along the track

Through the field
Mighty train
CLICKETY-CLACK
Along the track

Onto the trestle
Over the river

CLICKETY-CLACK

Along the track

Up the mountain
'Round the bend

ANIMAS
RIVER
ELEV. 7200 FT.

CH-CH-CHOO

Heavy load

MORE STEAM!

HISSSSS

Through the town
Smoke swirls

WHOO-

WHOO-

WHOO

Whistle blows

Going back
Along the track

CLICKETY-CLACK

Along the track

At the station
Smokestack clean

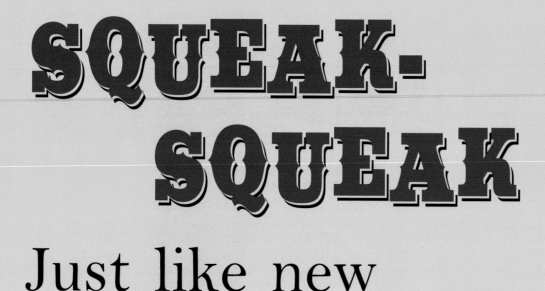

Just like new

Day ends
Turn the train

SHHH-SHHH

Rest stop

Ring the bell
All Aboard!

wHoo-
wHoo

Ready to go

TRAIN

THE TRAINS:

Unlike modern trains that use electricity, only coal and steam make these mighty engines move. That's why they are called "steam engines." Water is in the long, huge tube in the front part of the engine. Coal and even more water are stored behind it, in the tender.

The engineer and the fireman work in a cab at the back of the engine. The engineer makes the locomotive go forward, stop, and reverse. It's the fireman's job to give the engineer the power to make the train go. Everyone works together to be sure the journey is safe and fun.

Just like ships, it is a tradition to refer to the locomotives as "she" or "sister." The engineer says, "These old locomotives seem alive. They talk to each other. They set off little puffs of steam and burp and hiss."

The heaviest Durango & Silverton Narrow Gauge locomotive weighs 143 tons. She travels at a speed of eighteen miles per hour.

It takes six tons of coal to make a trip from Durango to Silverton and back. The fireman shovels all the coal by hand — twenty pounds at a time.

The engine's boiler is the big cylinder in the front of the locomotive. It has an oven that burns the coal to make the steam.

The boiler holds 2500 gallons of water in this engine and the tender holds 5000 gallons. The water is pumped from the tender to the boiler in front of the engine. It pumps 3500 gallons an hour.

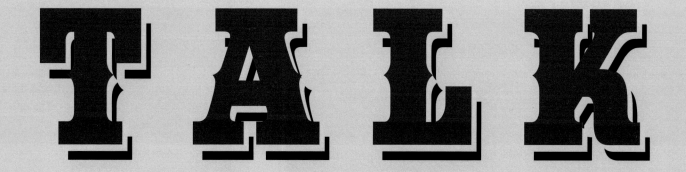

TALK

Water makes the steam to turn around the pistons. Pistons push the side rods to make the big wheels go.

The stack that sits on top of the engine has an air compressor to help the train breathe. In it is a "bear trap," a metal screen that helps to protect the environment. It catches ash and junk that would otherwise float into the air.

Steam locomotives have two wheels in front, eight driving wheels, and two wheels in the back.

THE TRACKS:
"Gauge" is the width of a railroad track. Narrow gauge tracks are three feet wide while standard gauge for modern trains is four-and-a-half feet, the historic width of a Roman chariot.

THE WHISTLES:
All trains, standard and narrow gauge, blow the same whistles.
- Two long whistles means the train is ready to go.
- Two long whistles, a short one, and another long one means the train is approaching a crossing.
- One short whistle means apply brakes and stop.
- Three short whistles when the train is not moving means back up, and when the train is moving means that it will stop at the next station.

To learn more about the Durango & Silverton Narrow Gauge Railroad,
check out the website at www.durangotrain.com

FOR BAILEY, WITH LOVE.

THE AUTHOR WOULD LIKE TO THANK KRISTI NELSON-COHEN; THE STAFF AND VOLUNTEERS AT THE D&SNGRR; MARSHALL NORSTEIN; AND HER BROTHER-IN-LAW, TRAIN ENTHUSIAST EXTRAORDINAIRE, VICTOR KUKLIN.